NASCAR

Rachel Eagen

x1000r/min

CRABTREE PUBLISHING COMPANY
www.crabtreebooks.com

Crabtree Publishing Company
www.crabtreebooks.com

In loving memory of Wilf Secord

Coordinating editor: Ellen Rodger
Editors: Carrie Gleason, Adrianna Morganelli, L. Michelle Nielsen
Design and production coordinator: Rosie Gowsell
Cover design and production assistance: Samara Parent
Art direction: Rob MacGregor
Scanning technician: Arlene Arch-Wilson
Photo research: Allison Napier

Consultants: Andrew Elliott; Norm Mort, automotive historian and journalist

Photo Credits: AP/Wide World Photos: p. 19, p. 21 (top), p. 24, p. 28 (left), p. 31 (top front and bottom); Bettmann/Corbis: p. 6, p. 7 (both), p. 10, p. 28 (right); Duomo/Corbis: p. 30 (bottom behind); Harold Hinson/TSN/ZUMA/Corbis: cover, p. 5 (top); Robert Holmes/Corbis: p. 23; Michael Kim/Corbis: p. 5 (bottom); Reuters/Corbis: p. 17 (bottom), p. 29 (both); Phil Schermeister/Corbis: p. 13;

Sam Sharpe/Corbis: p. 17 (top), p. 20, p. 25 (bottom), p. 26; Sam Sharpe/www.thesharpeimage.com/The Sharpe Image/Corbis: p. 15 (top); William R. Sallaz/NewSport/Corbis: p. 30 (bottom front); George Tiedemann/GT Images/Corbis: p. 1, p. 4, p. 12; George Tiedemann/NewSport/Corbis: p. 11, p. 14, p. 15 (bottom), p. 16, pp.18-19, p. 21 (bottom), p. 22, p. 25 (top), p. 27 (top), p. 31 (top behind); Motorsports Images & Archives Photography. Used with permission: p. 8, p. 9, p. 27 (bottom). Other images from stock CD.

Cover: Cars bank on a turn during the Dickies 500 at Texas Motor Speedway. The bold colors, sponsorship decals, and numbers make each driver's ride easy for NASCAR fans to identify.

Title page: NASCAR is the fastest growing sport in the United States. Fans flock to races each weekend to see their favorite drivers race cars at speeds of more than 160 miles per hour (257 kilometers per hour).

Library and Archives Canada Cataloguing in Publication

Eagen, Rachel, 1979-
  NASCAR / Rachel Eagen.

(Automania!)
Includes index.
ISBN-13: 978-0-7787-3007-1 (bound)
ISBN-10: 0-7787-3007-7 (bound)
ISBN-13: 978-0-7787-3029-3 (pbk.)
ISBN-10: 0-7787-3029-8 (pbk.)

  1. NASCAR (Association)--Juvenile literature. 2. Stock car racing--United States--Juvenile literature. I. Title. II. Series.

GV1029.9.S74E24 2006   j796.720973   C2006-902457-X

Library of Congress Cataloging-in-Publication Data

Eagen, Rachel, 1979-
  NASCAR / written by Rachel Eagen.

    p. cm. -- (Automania!)
Includes index.
ISBN-13: 978-0-7787-3007-1 (rlb)
ISBN-10: 0-7787-3007-7 (rlb)
ISBN-13: 978-0-7787-3029-3 (pb)
ISBN-10: 0-7787-3029-8 (pb)
  1. Stock car racing--United States--Juvenile literature. 2. NASCAR (Association)--Juvenile literature. I. Title. II. Series.
    GV1029.9.S74E24 2006
    796.720973--dc22

                                          2006012406

Crabtree Publishing Company

www.crabtreebooks.com   1-800-387-7650

Published in Canada
Crabtree Publishing
616 Welland Ave.
St. Catharines, ON
L2M 5V6

Published in the United States
Crabtree Publishing
PMB16A
350 Fifth Ave., Suite 3308
New York, NY 10118

Published in the United Kingdom
Crabtree Publishing
White Cross Mills
High Town, Lancaster
LA1 4XS

Published in Australia
Crabtree Publishing
386 Mt. Alexander Rd.
Ascot Vale (Melbourne)
VIC 3032

Contents

Start Your Engines!

NASCAR racing is one of the most popular sports in the United States with hundreds of races held each year. Each weekend, thousands of fans crowd stadiums at NASCAR races to cheer on their favorite drivers and teams.

The Love of Speed

Stock car racing is the fastest growing sport in the United States. Fans are lured to racetracks by the smell of burnt rubber, the sound of screeching tires, and the rumble of the engines as the cars race by. Stock cars race at speeds approaching 200 miles per hour (322 kilometers per hour).

(above) Fans cheer at the opening lap of the Coca-Cola 600, one of many NASCAR races.

Stock, but Better

Stock cars look like regular sedans, or passenger cars, but they are very different. Stock cars have specially designed engines and **modified** bodies that give them speed and stability on the track. Stock cars do not include many of the features that regular passenger cars have, including speedometers, back seats, side-view mirrors, headlights, stereos, or even doors.

Making it Official

NASCAR is the short form for the National Association for Stock Car Auto Racing. NASCAR is an association of stock car racing teams and their owners, as well as the officials who make decisions about changes to the rule book. NASCAR officials create a set of rules that drivers and cars must follow at every race. NASCAR races operate on a points system. Drivers earn points for how well they "run," or drive in each race, and how many wins they take each season. The driver with the most points at the end of the season is declared the NASCAR National Champion.

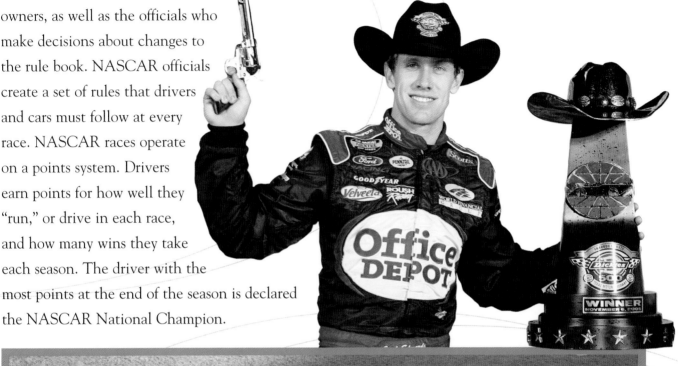

Driver Carl Edwards celebrates his win in Texas style in a NEXTEL Cup series race at the Texas Motor Speedway.

Driver Dale Earnhardt Jr. does a doughnut in the infield of Daytona International Speedway after winning the Daytona 500 race in 2004.

Early Days of Racing

The first mass produced **automobiles** hit the streets of North America by the early 1900s, and the sport of auto racing soon followed. Those early races were rough by today's standards, with cars barreling around dirt tracks, driving fast from city to city, or even testing their speed on sandy beaches.

Have Car, Will Race

In 1908, American car maker Henry Ford built the Model T. The Model T was the first low-priced American mass produced family car. Cars changed the way people lived. As more people bought cars, there was a need for paved roads, as well as gas stations, and garages for people to keep their cars in when they were not being driven.

The first American auto race was held in 1895 from Chicago to Waukegan, Illinois. The Vanderbilt Cup (above), first held in 1904, was one of the first major organized American car races.

Race Ya!

By the early 1900s, car racing was becoming popular throughout North America. New car makes and models appeared, and American manufacturers raced them in Europe and Britain. Companies began to manufacture **runabouts,** or speedsters, which soon appeared at informal races, or races that were not organized, throughout the United States. More formal races were **sanctioned** by the **American Automobile Association**. Drivers began making minor changes to their cars, known as modifications. They did things such as removing their front fenders and headlights to make the cars lighter, faster, and to prevent glass from shattering.

The First Tracks

In the early days of racing, county fairgrounds were used as racetracks. Most fairgrounds had large, oval-shaped dirt tracks that were made for racing horses. Drivers also raced on the hard sand of Daytona Beach in Florida. Races attracted large excited crowds. Each track used a different set of rules. Drivers could race any kind of car they wanted and make modifications to them as they wished. This allowed some drivers to have an advantage over others.

(below) American car maker Henry Ford brought his six-cylinder Ford racer to a beach course in 1905 to test its speed.

Daytona Beach, Florida, was a favorite spot for many early car races and speed trials. The beach was a long, unbroken stretch of hard-packed sand that was wide enough for many cars.

The Birth of NASCAR

Stock car racing grew in popularity in the United States throughout the 1930s and 1940s. At first, there were no regulations, or official rules, or regularly scheduled races. Over time, stock car racing evolved into the regulated sport it is today.

Purse Races

By the 1930s, drivers were racing street-legal sedans at informal races. Daytona Beach, a wide stretch of hard ocean sand in Florida, formed the course for a 78-lap race in 1936. A $1,700 prize went to the winner, but the organizers lost money on the event. Stock car racing might have ended there if not for the determination of Bill France.

"Big Bill"

Bill France was an auto mechanic and driver who set up a garage in Florida in 1934. France organized car races by promoting them among garage owners and finding **sponsors** for prizes. He organized 10 races from 1937 to 1941 when **World War II** was declared and racing stopped. After the war, France pushed for an organization that would bring order and **uniformity** to racing.

Organizing the Sport

France wanted a race organization that would include one set of rules, a points system, and award an overall "national championship" to the driver who earned the most points. In 1947, France gathered together drivers and other stock car racing promoters for a meeting. The meeting resulted in the creation of the National Association for Stock Car Auto Racing, or NASCAR. NASCAR became the official governing body for the sport and France became NASCAR's first president.

The First Race

The first official NASCAR-sanctioned race took place just south of Daytona Beach, in 1948. It was a 150-mile (241-kilometer) race, with part of the track located on a stretch of beach. Over 14,000 fans attended the event, making the first NASCAR race a success.

Driver and garage owner Bill France became one of the founding fathers of NASCAR in 1947. His son Bill France Jr. and grandson Brian France followed in his footsteps.

The route for the Daytona Beach race ran along the beach, but only at low tide so that the cars would not be swept out to sea. Veteran dirt track driver Red Byron won the race.

New Standards, New Rules

NASCAR brought major changes to stock car racing, including a formal rule book. The rule book listed the kinds of car modifications that were allowed. Racetrack owners had to keep their tracks in good repair, and fix damages such as broken guardrails. An official racing schedule was created so that the same drivers could compete against each other at every race.

Stock, Modified, Roadsters

In 1948, NASCAR included three race classes: strictly stock, modified, and **roadsters**. Vehicles such as Buicks, Lincolns, and Fords competed in the first strictly stock race, held in Charlotte, North Carolina. Drivers rolled to the track in their family sedans, competed, then drove home in the same vehicles. Strictly stock was dropped because of a shortage of new full-sized American-built cars.

Built for Speed

As more people became interested in the sport of stock car racing, the cars became more powerful. Modifications included special tires for speed and roll cages to keep the drivers safe.

Street to Track

Up until the late 1950s, NASCAR drivers raced regular passenger sedans. These cars were not built for racing, so they required frequent repairs to the brakes and **suspension**. The tires were skinny and the rubber was too thin to hold up to the extreme heat that built up during a race. As a result, car tires were constantly blowing out. This threatened the safety of drivers, who easily lost control of their vehicles when a tire popped.

Early Improvements

Stock cars were altered to keep drivers safer during crashes. At first, hubcaps were removed. Hubcaps littered the tracks after accidents and damaged other cars. Headlights were also removed and replaced with stickers. In the 1950s, a roll cage was added to the **chassis**, or main body, of a car. Made of heavy-duty steel tubes, a roll cage runs inside the car over the top of the driver and is attached to the middle of the frame. If a car flips over in an accident, the roll cage prevents the roof from crumpling in on the driver.

A tire blowout caused driver Red Byron to lose control of his car and careen into a crowd of spectators during a race in the early days of stock cars. One spectator was killed and 16 others were injured in the accident. The tires used in those days often burst. Drivers often used a trap door in the floor of their compartment to check tire wear. In 1952, the Pure Oil Company began making racing tires for stock cars that could hold up to the high speeds on the dirt tracks.

Not So "Stock"

Stock cars are only partially made in factories today. Factories produce the bumper panels, windshield posts, floors, hoods, and trunks. Everything else, including the bodies, fenders, and **quarter panels**, are custom-made by each **racing team**. The cars are designed to be aerodynamic, or able to cut through the air, and travel at high speeds. There are switches and dials located on the **instrument panels** to help drivers control their cars. Stock cars have only one seat, the driver's seat. A driver must climb through the window to get into the car.

The Garage

Racing teams do most of their work in garages in the months, weeks, and days before a race. Teams follow NASCAR rules for body types, engine specifications, and safety regulations. Upwards of 40 workers design cars using computer programs and build them in the shop. Some racing teams have several cars of their own, plus ones they work on for other racing teams that do not have their own shops.

Racing Divisions

NASCAR sanctions, or approves, several different racing divisions that run thousands of races on hundreds of tracks every year. Each division runs racing series, or groups of races that drivers participate in while following NASCAR rules. Each racing series features different vehicles and track styles.

National Racing

The biggest and most popular NASCAR races fall within the National Division. This division features three racing series: the Busch Series, the NEXTEL Cup Series, and the Craftsman Truck Series. Each series has its own rules for vehicle size, modifications, and parts that can be used. The cars in the Busch Series are lighter and have less horsepower than those in the NEXTEL Cup Series.

The NEXTEL Cup Series, formerly known as the NASCAR Winston Cup Series, features the top drivers of the sport. NEXTEL Cup Series races attract a larger audience because they feature the best drivers and are often shown on television.

NASCAR's National Division Craftsman Truck Series features professional drivers in modified pickup trucks.

Grand National Racing

The Grand National Division features two racing series, the Busch North and the Winston West series. Busch North races are held on tracks in the northern United States, including Maine, Massachusetts, New Hampshire, New York, Pennsylvania, and Connecticut. The NASCAR Winston West Series is one of NASCAR's longest running series, with the first race dating back to 1954. Winston West races are held on tracks in the western United States, including California, Colorado, Nevada, Arizona, Washington, and Oregon. The cars that race in both Grand National series are slightly more lightweight than those in the National series, and car engines are less powerful.

(above) A crew repairs an engine in Cedarville, California. Good stock "shops" and pit crews are vital at all levels of competition.

Elite Racing Division

There are four racing series within the Elite Racing Division, covering specific regions of the United States: the Southwest, Southeast, Midwest, and Northwest series. The Northwest Series features races in Oregon and Washington. Drivers usually gain experience at this level and move on to higher-level racing, including the Grand National and National series. The cars at this racing level are less powerful than those that compete at the Grand National level, so they do not go as fast.

Weekly Racing Series

The NASCAR Weekly Racing Series is the lowest level of NASCAR competition, but it is an important racing series because it allows drivers to gain racing experience and fine-tune their driving skills. The drivers at this level are mostly funded by local sponsors, rather than well-known corporations.

A Day at the Races

Most NASCAR National Division races are held on Sunday afternoons, and they are watched on television by millions of fans across North America. Teams prepare for several days before each race, and every team must enter a qualifying round before race day.

Qualifying

Qualifying rounds are held a few days before race day. The qualifying round determines which drivers will compete, and their starting position in the race. Drivers race a car with a qualifying engine. The drivers with the fastest laps are placed at the start of the pack on race day.

The green flag is waved at the start of the Coca-Cola 600 at Lowe's Motor Speedway.

Start Your Engines!

At the beginning of each race, NASCAR drivers take several warm-up laps around the track behind a pace car. The pace car leads the pack, guiding the drivers around the track and gradually working the cars up to their racing speeds. Drivers use this time to determine how well their cars are handling and whether any adjustments to the steering or suspension are required. Once everyone is lined up and driving according to qualifying times, the pace car darts off the track, the green flag is dropped, and the race begins.

(left) Jeff Gordon's pit crew refuels the car and changes tires during a race. Crews wear protective equipment such as fire-protective clothing and helmets.

(below) Light towers display the number of laps, usually at the top, and the car numbers in the order they are racing. The numbers change quickly.

Pit Road

Each race runs about four to five hours, depending on how many miles are covered. The cars cannot go for this long without making pit stops to change tires, fill up with gas, and make minor repairs. Pit road is a strip inside the track, where drivers go several times throughout a race. Larger repairs, such as fixing a car's suspension, must be made off the track. This is called going behind the wall.

The Pit Crew

A pit crew can help a driver win or lose a race. Pit stops must be perfectly coordinated. An extra second or two can mean the difference between winning and losing a race. Most pit stops last 15 seconds or less. Some pit crews practice pit stops for up to an hour every day. Each pit crew member has a different job. The jack person uses a jack to lift the car up on one side while tire carriers roll new tires in place. Tire changers use power tools to remove the old tires and fasten new ones onto the car. The gas-can person refuels the car, while the catch-can person holds a device to catch any fuel before it spills on the track. The crew chief is in charge of the pit crew and communicates with the driver on a radio system. Race day crew members, such as spotters and engineers, watch the car on the track and report problems to the crew chief.

The Races

Individual races are sometimes named after large corporate sponsors, or the name of the track, and they usually feature the number of miles involved in the race. For example, the Coca-Cola 600, sponsored by Coca-Cola, is a 600-mile (965-kilometer) race. It is the longest NASCAR race, and is held at Lowe's Motor Speedway in Concord, North Carolina. The Daytona 500 is the most important race in the NASCAR NEXTEL Cup Series. It is a 500-mile (805-kilometer) race in Daytona Beach, Florida. The Daytona-500 kicks off the racing season each year in February. It is known as "The Great American Race."

(above) The flagman waves the green flag at drivers at the start of a NASCAR race.

The Flagman

The flagman stands over the starting line, which is also the finish line, and communicates messages to the drivers using various colored flags. Here is what some of them mean:

Green = Go. The green flag signals the start of the race.

Yellow = Caution. Drivers must slow down because the track is unsafe.

Black = The driver must go to the pits because there is something wrong with his or her car. The black flag is also waved for bad driving.

Red = Stop. This flag usually warns drivers of a dangerous situation on the track, such as an accident or a rain delay. All cars must stop no matter where they are on the track.

White = The lead car is on its final lap.

Blue with a yellow diagonal stripe = The driver must yield to a car that is about to pass.

Checkered = The winner has crossed the finish line.

Victory Lane

Victory Lane is a separate section of the course where drivers head after winning a race. After winning, most drivers take a lap or two to cool off, wave to the fans, and do doughnuts on the frontstretch or in the infield. Meanwhile, TV crews wait in Victory Lane to congratulate, interview, and take pictures of the winner.

Sponsors

Running a NASCAR team is very expensive, so teams rely on sponsors to help out with some of the costs. Sponsors are the businesses and corporations who provide funding to NASCAR teams. In exchange for giving the team money, the team advertises for their sponsors by wearing T-shirts, hats, and other items that have the sponsors' logos on them. The major sponsors of a team are obvious because the car itself is plastered with the logos, and painted with a color scheme to match. Sponsors also appear on the driver's driving suit, and on the driver's helmet.

Driver Jimmie Johnson hoists a hefty belt in truimph on Victory Lane. Drivers also traditionally spray champagne over the crowd.

Race day is a family affair for many fans. These youngsters cool off in their makeshift pool in the back of a pickup in the infield of the Daytona International Speedway before the Pepsi 400.

Life in the Fast Lane

Stock cars are made to have as little air resistance as possible so they can race around the track at top speeds. Their engines are larger and more powerful than the engines in passenger cars, and their tires are designed to be light so they do not explode at high speeds.

Spoilers

The spoiler is a long metal wing that stretches across the rear end of the car. It sticks up like a fin. As air flows toward the back of the car, it collects in front of the spoiler. This creates downward pressure on the car and forces it to hug the track, helping the car to go faster. The spoiler stabilizes the car by preventing the back end from lifting up.

Suspension

The suspension is made up of springs, shock absorbers, and other parts that are connected to the wheels and axles of the car. Suspension affects how well a car **handles**. NASCAR stock cars have independent suspension in the front. This means that the front wheels function separately from each other, giving the driver more control. In the back, the left and right wheels are on a common axle.

What in Tirenation?

Some tracks pitch used NASCAR Goodyear race tires over the fence to fans as after-race souvenirs. Each team is given several tires and the tires are prepared and set out for easy access before race day. Cars run through 16 or more tires per race.

Piston Power

Teams use more powerful engines for qualifying rounds and replace them on race day with engines that last longer. Most teams have several engines for each car. Stock car engines can easily be placed in and taken out of a car. Pistons fire the car's crankshaft, which make thousands of revolutions per minute, and in turn, work the car's wheels and axles.

Air Dam

An air dam is attached to the front bumper and hangs down so that it almost touches the ground. It helps a car to be more aerodynamic by blocking and forcing the flow of air to the sides and over the top of the car. The air dam also helps keep the front end of the car stable.

Tires

NASCAR vehicles use special, heavy-duty tires. The tires do not have treads, which helps to increase **traction** on racetracks. The tires are about 12 inches (30 centimeters) wide and are much lighter than regular tires. Each tire has two layers: a metal rim, and a rubber outer layer. Tires are changed about four times during a race and the tire pressure varies according to race conditions, such as extreme heat or wet tracks.

22

Get Your Motor Running

The engine is the part of the car that produces power. It is like the heart of the car, because without the engine, the car would not be able to move. A stock car engine is about four times more powerful than the engine of an ordinary car.

Powerhouse

Engine specialists study, design, and test stock car engines to make them powerful, durable, or long-lasting, and efficient. An engine's power is measured in units called horsepower (hp), which are produced by the pumping action of cylinders within the engine. Most ordinary cars have engines with either four or six cylinders. Stock car engines have eight cylinders and create 750 to 800 horsepower. The powerful engines allow the cars to go close to 200 miles per hour (322 kilometers per hour) for up to five hours at a time.

Carburetor Restrictor Plates

On some tracks, teams must use carburetor restrictor plates to keep drivers from racing faster than 200 miles per hour (322 kilometers per hour). A carburetor restrictor plate is a square of metal that fits under the **carburetor** of an engine. It cuts down on the amount of air sucked into the engine, reducing the engine's horsepower. While higher speeds are more exciting for fans, they are more dangerous for drivers. Before restrictor plates were introduced, stock cars ran over 210 miles per hour (338 kilometers per hour).

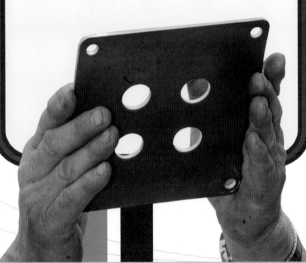

NASCAR officials measure carburetor restrictor plates at some tracks. Restrictor plates limit the amount of air that can enter a car's engine. Less air means less horsepower, and slower and safer race speeds.

Qualifying Engine

NASCAR teams use more powerful engines for qualifying rounds, so that their cars can reach the highest possible speeds, and hopefully get the best starting position on race day. Qualifying engines are lighter in weight than regular racing engines, giving them more power. These qualifying engines are built for speed rather than endurance, which is why they last only a few laps around the track before dying. After qualifying, the engine is removed and replaced with a more durable and reliable one.

(below) NASCAR race cars fuel up at the infield gas station during the Banquet 400, a NEXTEL Cup Series race, at the Kansas Speedway.

NASCAR Tracks

There are three basic styles of tracks in NASCAR racing. They are superspeedways, short tracks, and intermediate tracks. NASCAR stock cars also sometimes race on road courses, which do not have a definite shape, and feature tight turns and some embankments.

Superspeedways

Superspeedways are paved courses that are at least 2.5 miles (four kilometers) long. Superspeedways are tri-oval shaped, which makes them look a little bit like a giant "D." All cars are required to have carburetor restrictor plates on their engines for superspeedway races. Cars travel at almost 200 miles per hour (322 kilometers per hour) on flat, straight stretches, but at lower speeds on corners.

NASCAR short tracks include Bristol Motor Speedway (above), Martinsville Speedway, and Richmond International Raceway.

Short Tracks

Short tracks are less than one mile (1.6 kilometers) long. Drivers race in a much tighter pack on short tracks because there is less room for them to maneuver around each other. This causes the cars to bump and scrape together, so accidents are far more frequent on short tracks than on superspeedways. Short tracks may be high-banked, but some of them are not. On short tracks, teams use tires that have a second rubber layer that sits inside the outside layer. This helps the drivers maintain control of their cars if blowouts occur.

Intermediate Tracks

Intermediate tracks are often oval-shaped and between one mile (1.6 kilometers) and two miles (three kilometers) long. Intermediate tracks may or may not be banked, and come in a variety of shapes other than the popular oval. For example, Darlington Raceway in Darlington, South Carolina, is egg-shaped, while Pocono Raceway in Long Pond, Pennsylvania, is triangular.

(above) The Sears Point International Raceway is a road course that challenges drivers.

Road Courses

Road courses are combination tracks that include tight and gradual turns, as well as embankments and flat stretches. They usually involve several left and right turns, which require the drivers to slow down and change gears. Sears Point International Raceway is an 11-turn course less than two miles (three kilometers) long in Sonoma, California. Watkins Glen International in Watkins Glen, New York, is almost 2.5 miles (four kilometers) long, and also features 11 turns.

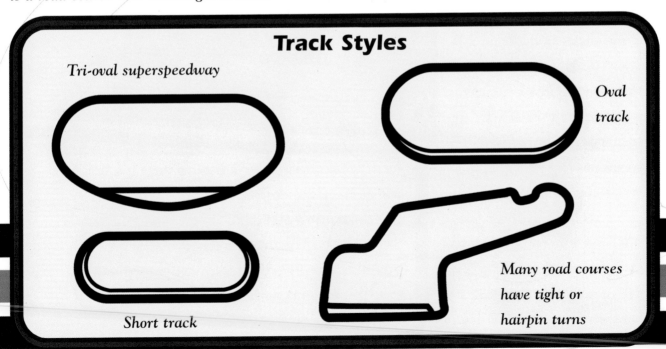

Track Styles

Tri-oval superspeedway

Oval track

Short track

Many road courses have tight or hairpin turns

Car Safety

Stock car racing is a dangerous sport. Crashes are common, and many drivers suffer several injuries during their racing careers. Over the years, there have been many improvements to cars, tracks, and driver equipment that have made the sport safer.

Fire

Fire used to be a big problem in the early days of NASCAR. Fuel tanks easily ruptured when cars crashed into walls or other cars, causing the cars to explode into giant fireballs. Today, NASCAR fuel cells, or fuel tanks are made of steel with a rubber container filled with foam. This is so the fuel does not slosh around and the tank will not explode or be easily **punctured** in an accident. Special walls separate the main body from the back end, and from the engine at the front of the car. This protects the driver from flames if a fire starts under the hood or in the back. Cars are also equipped with fire extinguishers located within the driver's reach. If a fire spreads to the car's interior, the driver has the equipment to put it out. Usually, drivers try to get out of their cars as quickly as possible, rather than worry about putting the fire out.

A car breaks apart after crashing near the finish line at Daytona International Speedway in 1999. The car barrel-rolled eight times. Every piece of the car's body had been sheared off by the time it stopped. The driver, Jeff Bagwell, pulled himself from the car and was not seriously injured.

Some NASCAR tracks use soft wall technology to lessen the danger of crashes. Inside barrier walls' soft material, such as foam or water, absorbs the impact of crashing cars.

Flip Out

Roll bars and roll cages are important features that help keep a driver safe. A roll cage is made of steel tubing that surrounds the driver. It protects the driver from being crushed if the car slams into a wall, another car, or is rear-ended. The driver's seat is designed to prevent the driver from bouncing around if the car spins or rolls. Side extensions curve around the driver's body and head to make a snug fit. NASCAR teams have fabricators who customize car chassis. Cars must pass safety inspections to be track approved.

Broken Glass

Stock cars were once raced just as they were made in factories, but today's specially designed vehicles do not have any glass, because it easily breaks and could seriously hurt the driver in an accident. The car windshields and back windows are made from a hard, shatterproof plastic called Lexan. Decals replace glass headlights and taillights so that they cannot shatter. Strong nylon netting replaces the driver's window. The driver can quickly release the netting with a push of a button in order to exit the car in a hurry.

Roof flaps lie flat while the car is moving forward, but pop up when the car spins sideways or backwards. They help to prevent the car from lifting up into the air during an accident.

Car and Driver Gear

At one time, NASCAR drivers raced in street clothes without safety equipment. Today, cars and tracks are designed to be as safe as possible. Drivers wear special gear to protect them in accidents, and use equipment such as heat shields and hydration systems to cope with the blistering hot temperatures inside the cars.

Buckle Up

Seat belts are one of the most important aspects of driver safety. Stock cars have five-point seat belts. Unlike ordinary passenger cars, in which the seat belt crosses the lap and chest of the driver, five-point seat belts strap over the driver's lap, over each shoulder, and through the driver's legs. They are called racing harnesses. It is important that the driver is prevented from moving as much as possible to prevent injury. The seat belts are made to fit very tightly.

Helmets and HANS

All drivers wear helmets that are custom-made to perfectly fit their heads. The helmets have full-face shields to protect their faces from flying debris if there is an accident. A collar known as HANS, or "head-and-neck-support," is a harness that the driver wears on his or her upper body and attaches to the back of the helmet and seat. HANS collars keep the driver's head from snapping sideways or forward if the car jerks or crashes.

Driver Jeff Gordon wears fire-resistant long underwear and a full-body outer suit. Fireproof boots protect the driver's feet. Some drivers also wear heat shields over the tops of their feet and under their heels. Heat shields are reflective pads that protect the driver's feet from blistering from the heat of the pedals and floorboards. Special fireproof gloves protect the driver's hands and allow him or her to grip the steering wheel for several hours.

(above) NASCAR driver Tony Stewart is wearing a HANS collar, a safety device that can help save a driver's life during a crash. His hands are protected by fireproof gloves.

Cages and Walls

Today's stock cars are built around a frame containing a steel roll cage. The sturdy and strong roll cage surrounds the driver's compartment and protects the driver in a crash. A steel **firewall** separates the engine from the driver's compartment and also protects the driver from engine fires. Many NASCAR tracks now use soft wall technology to make crashes safer. Soft wall technology means the walls lining the inside of the track are made from soft materials, such as foam, that absorb the impact of cars crashing against them.

In the early days of stock car racing, drivers had little protection in crashes. Here driver Ralph Earnheardt wears goggles and a helmet. His driving "suit" is a mechanic's uniform.

Long May You Run

There have been many great drivers and driving families in the history of NASCAR. They devoted their lives to the sport, following grueling weekly schedules of training and racing.

Bobby Allison

Bobby Allison was born in Miami, Florida, in 1937, and began racing when he was just 18 years old. By the end of his career in 1997, Allison had taken home 85 NASCAR victories. Known as an aggressive driver, Allison is remembered for having a fistfight with another driver, Cale Yarborough, on the infield of the Daytona 500 in 1979. Bobby Allison's career ended after crashing his car in 1998. He survived the accident, but he never raced again. Allison's sons Davey and Clifford were also NASCAR drivers. Davey died in a helicopter crash in 1992 and Clifford died during a practice run at Michigan Speedway.

Richard Petty

Richard Petty is considered the king of stock car racing. Petty's father, Lee, was a top NASCAR driver who won the first Daytona 500 race in 1959. Petty's brother Maurice built the engines that brought his brother success. Richard entered the NASCAR circuit in 1958 at the age of 21, and began winning races just one year into his career. He retired from racing in 1992, having won seven NASCAR National Championships. Richard's son, Kyle, is also a NASCAR driver. His grandson Adam continued the family racing tradition but died in a track accident in 2000.

(above) NASCAR was always a highly charged, emotional sport. Drivers Bobby Allison and Cale Yarborough mix it up after a race in 1979.

(right) Richard Petty celebrates winning the Winston 500 with his wife, Linda. Four generations of the Petty family have been NASCAR drivers.

Fans miss Number 3, Dale Earnhardt, who died in 2001. His son Dale Jr. races with Dale Earnhardt Incorporated, which now funds three NASCAR NEXTEL Cup teams. Many NASCAR families have helped to make the sport famous.

The Earnhardts

Dale Earnhardt was born in Kannapolis, North Carolina, in 1951. His father Ralph, was a NASCAR Sportsman champion. Dale joined the NASCAR circuit in 1975 and won 76 NASCAR Cups, driving a black Chevy, for which he became known as "The Man in Black." Earnhardt earned another nickname for himself, "The Master of the Draft," because of his ability to pass other cars on the track. Unfortunately, Dale Earnhardt's career was cut short when he was killed in an accident at the Daytona 500 in 2001. No other driver has used Earnhardt's Number 3 since his death, and NASCAR is considering retiring the number permanently in Earnhardt's honor. One of Earnhardt's sons, Dale Jr., is also a top NASCAR driver. Dale Jr. began his racing career at age 17 at Concord, North Carolina.

He took home the Busch Series championship in 1998, his first year competing at the NASCAR National level. Dale Jr. repeated his performance in 1999. Earnhardt, or "Little E," as he is known to his fans, entered the NASCAR Winston Cup Series in 2000. Off the track, Dale Jr. promotes NASCAR by appearing on television talk shows, and this has attracted a new audience to stock car racing.

Jeff Gordon

Jeff Gordon is considered by many to be the best NASCAR driver today. Gordon showed natural talent for racing as a teenager, and began competing in short track races when he was only 17 years old. Since taking home his first NASCAR Cup in 1995, Gordon's Number 24 car has become a common sight in Victory Lane, averaging around six racing victories per year. Gordon fans eagerly collect trading cards, T-shirts, and the Jeff Gordon action figure, which was released in 2003. Many compare Jeff Gordon to NASCAR legends Richard Petty and Dale Earnhardt.

Driver Jeff Gordon started his racing career early. As a youngster, he raced go-carts and moved on to NASCAR in 1992.

Elliott Sadler

Elliott Sadler started racing go-carts at age seven. He showed promise as a Late Model Stock driver, and began making a name for himself in 1993, when he won 13 races in the Dodge weekly racing series. By 1995, Sadler moved into Busch Series racing. He won his first Cup race in 2001 at Bristol Motor Speedway. Beginning the race in 38th place, Sadler took a big risk by skipping a pit stop, giving him the opportunity to move ahead and win. Sadler's Number 38 Ford is easily spotted on the track because of its candy-colored paint scheme, showing his main sponsor, M&M's.

Sweet tooth? Driver Elliott Sadler's suit and Ford are plastered with the candy logos of his sponsor. His brother Hermie is also a NASCAR driver.

The Women of NASCAR

NASCAR is a male-dominated sport, but a few women have broken this tradition. Louise Smith competed in stock car races from 1946 to 1956. She won 39 races, and in 1999, she became the first woman to be inducted into the International Motorsports Hall of Fame. Janet Guthrie was the first woman to compete in the NASCAR Winston Cup Series in 1976, where she finished 15th in the World 600 race. Guthrie was one of the first women inducted into the International Women's Sports Hall of Fame. Shawna Robinson entered the NASCAR Winston Cup Series in 2002. She was voted Rookie of the Year in the 1988 NASCAR Dash Series. Robinson has set new standards, such as her track record speed of 184 miles per hour (296 kilometers per hour) at Michigan Speedway in 2000. Robinson also races in the NASCAR Craftsman Truck Series.

Janet Guthrie posted top ten finishes in both Indy Cars and the NASCAR Winston Cup, now the NEXTEL Cup. She was a top rookie in five Winston Cup races, and finished sixth in the 1977 race at Bristol Motorspeedway.

Glossary

American Automobile Association An organization formed in 1902 to promote the use of automobiles

carburetor A device in an engine that produces a mixture of vaporized fuel and air

chassis The steel frame of a car, its suspension, and running gear

debris Loose or scattered litter, or fragments from a wreck

doughnut A fast, tight circular turn often made by race winners in the infield or on Victory Lane

firewall A barrier used to stop fire from spreading

handles How a car corners and rides while driving

instrument panels A group of instruments on a car's dashboard

mass produce To make large amounts of one product, usually using automated machines

modified Altered or changed to make an improvement

punctured Something that is pierced or has a hole in it, such as a tire

quarter panels The panels or sides of a car

racing team A team that has an owner and/or sponsors and runs a car or many cars in NASCAR races

roadsters An open two-seater automobile

runabout A small, lightweight automobile that often had only two seats

sanction Approval given by an official group

sponsors A person or company that finances, or gives money, to a racing team to help it with the expense of running cars, and paying team members and drivers in races

suspension A system of springs and other mechanical devices that insulate the car from the shocks that are delivered through the wheels in ordinary driving and racing

traction The friction that makes a car's tires stick to the track

uniformity Something that follows the same rules and keeps a level of sameness

World War II An international conflict or war that involved many countries and changed the world. It took place from 1939 to 1945

Index

Printed in the U.S.A.